Old BEXHILL

by
Charles Kaye

To M.C.K. and C.F.K.

First published in the United Kingdom, 2002,
by Stenlake Publishing
Telephone / Fax: 01290 551122

ISBN 1 84033 188 7

FURTHER READING

Anyone writing about Bexhill's history owes an immense debt to L. J. Bartley and his excellent account of the town's development. Other books listed have also been helpful in furnishing both background and detail. Please note that none of these titles are available from Stenlake Publishing. Those interested in finding out more are advised to contact their local bookshop or reference library.

The Story of Bexhill, L. J. Bartley, F. J. Parsons, Bexhill, 1971
Bexhill's Second Millennium Experience, D. A. Searson, Bexhill Museum Association, Bexhill, 2000
Earl De La Warr and the Competition for the Bexhill Pavilion, 1933–4, Russell Stevens and Peter Willis, Architectural History, vol. 33, 1990
Bexhill's Maharajah, Phyllis Burl, Bexhill Museum Association, 1998
St Mary Magdalene's Parish Centenary, Barnes Watson Press, Bexhill, 1993
The Story of St Peter's, Bexhill, Clifford Earwaker, 1997 (third edition)
A Walk in Bexhill Old Town, F. E. Rye, Old Town Preservation Society, n.d.
Bexhill-on-Sea, its Beginning, the People and District, H. G. Carey, Bexhill, 1983
Bexhill Voices, ed. Fred Gray, University of Sussex, 1994
Bexhill Voices Two, ed. Aylwin Guilmont, Bexhill-on-Sea, 1999
Lords and Landlords – the Aristocracy and the Towns 1774–1967, David Cannadine, Leicester University Press, 1980
Adolf Hitler: My Part in his Downfall, Spike Milligan, Penguin Books, 1972
Brands to Bexhill, Max Le Grand, Bookmarque, 1995

The walnut tree was one of the principal landmarks in the Old Town. Until late in the nineteenth century it stood in the grounds of the Manor House, immediately behind a flint stone boundary wall. When the road – at the junction of Church Street and De La Warr Road – was widened the wall was demolished and the tree became an island round which the traffic flowed. It was eventually cut down and the stump removed in 1921. Wood from the tree was used to make a gavel employed at the laying of the commemorative stone of the town hall extension in 1908. The tree in the background stood in the grounds of Sea View House and survived until after the Second World War. A seat (now removed) was created from its stump. To the right is part of the Manor House, since demolished. The buildings on the left remain little changed today and several of them are still in use as shops.

INTRODUCTION

The history of Bexhill can be conveniently, if unevenly, divided into three periods. The first covers its existence from the dim recesses of prehistory – revealed in the nineteenth century discoveries of iguanadon fragments and primitive boats on the site of Egerton Park – through its Anglo-Saxon charter of 772, up to the 1880s. The second period sees the transformation of the town into a resort with a massive expansion of its facilities and a recentring to the south of the site on the hill on which the old town stands. The third era runs from the early 1960s, when the role of seaside resort began to crumble, through to the present day and witnesses the borough in the process of a search for a new identity.

Although there are fragmentary remains from earliest times – some of which can be seen in Bexhill's admirable museum – the key event generally accepted as marking the beginning of a history specific to Bexhill is the charter of 772, of which only a medieval copy, in Latin, remains. In the charter, Offa II, King of Mercia (and of Offa's Dyke fame) granted land to Bishop Oswald to build a church 'to save the praise of God and the honour of the Saints'. Three hundred years later, when William the Conqueror divided up the spoils of victory, he gave Bexhill, as part of the Rape of Hastings, to Robert, Count of Eu, who later added a tower to that Saxon church (St Peter's).

The church held the manor of Bexhill until the mid-sixteenth century when Elizabeth I acquired it (as monarchs did) and in 1590 granted it to Thomas Sackville of Buckhurst who was created Earl of Dorset in 1603. He also held the large estate of Knole in Kent.

Little disturbed the rhythm of agricultural life until the Napoleonic wars brought with them a string of Martello towers along the south coast (to help counter any French invasion) and the billeting in Bexhill of the King's German Legion, whose barracks covered a wide area from the Old Town towards Sidley. There were twelve Martello towers between Galley Hill and the parish's western boundary and only one of these now survives, at Norman's Bay. The towers were named after Mortella Bay in Corsica where a similar structure had resisted British attacks. One of the demolished towers furnished some building material for St Mark's Church in Little Common.

By the mid-nineteenth century the Sackville family estates had passed to two sisters, Mary and Elizabeth, as co-heiresses, the younger of whom had married the 5th Earl De La Warr in 1813. The Buckhurst (including Bexhill) and Knole estates were later separated, going to different branches of the family. It was Elizabeth's grandson, the 7th Earl De La Warr, who started the transformation of Bexhill from country village to seaside resort.

George IV, when Prince of Wales, started the trend for seaside recreation on the south coast with his patronage of Brighton in the early 1800s and the building of the Regency Pavilion. The 1873 Ordnance Survey of Bexhill shows a cluster of dwellings around St Peter's in the Old Town and an adjacent group of houses in Belle Hill. There are virtually no buildings between the Old Town and the railway line, which had been opened in 1846 – only the coastguard station (on the site of the modern De La Warr Pavilion) and one house lay between the railway line and the sea.

In the nineteenth century, aristocratic families were responsible for the development of a number of south coast seaside resorts including Torquay, Folkestone and Bournemouth. The Dukes of Devonshire developed Eastbourne and the 7th and 8th Earls De La Warr created modern Bexhill. Between 1885 and 1900 the De La Warrs invested £50,000 (a considerable fortune) in the development of the town, and their influence lasted until World War II with the eponymous pavilion as their last achievement.

Development started in the early 1880s with the building of shops and houses in London Road (then known as Station Road), and in the area west of Holliers Hill. In 1881 the Metropolitan Convalescent Institution opened at the top of Sea Road on the edge of the Old Town. Residential building was also taking place in Hastings Road at the same time. Most significantly, work started on a sea wall and esplanade between Galley Hill and Sea Lane (later Sea Road) in 1883. Although the De La Warr estate originally envisaged development on the east side of town, progress there was spasmodic until the later 1890s when Dorset, Manor and Magdalen Roads were laid out and the Kursaal was built.

During the 1880s John Webb, the London building contractor who had been employed to construct the East Esplanade, started to develop the land he'd received in part payment. He laid out Western Road and built the Devonshire Hotel (of which he was the first licensee in 1886). The expansion of the area south of the railway followed, creating a new Bexhill and moving the centre of gravity firmly southwards. In 1884 the 7th Earl De La Warr added the suffix 'on Sea' to Bexhill. The town was expanding rapidly, with a population of 5,602 recorded in 1891 and 12,213 in 1901. In 1887 the *Bexhill-on-Sea Chronicle* was the first local newspaper to be established, followed by the *Bexhill-on-Sea Observer* in 1896. The construction of the Bexhill West to Crowhurst branch railway line in 1902 (closed by Beeching's axe in 1964) led to the building of the Pelham and Sussex Hotels in Sidley. Development to the west – in the Cranston and Collington estates – was also prompted by the opening of Bexhill West station, while the 8th Earl De La Warr developed the Cooden area with the Cooden Beach Golf Club, which opened in 1912.

Significantly, the development of independent schools flourished. The area around Hastings Road was particularly favoured: Harewood (later part of Charters Towers) opened there in 1887, and Ancaster House in 1898. These two schools, amalgamated in 1986, are now in Woodsgate Park. Schools were also set up in the Collington area, namely Seafield, Lake House, Effingham House and Falconbury (originally St Wilfrid's). This flourishing industry led in 1930 to the setting up of an Independent Schools Association. S. P. B. Mais, in his 1919 guide to Sussex, describes Bexhill as vying to be 'the centre of the best preparatory schools'.

Most hotel-building took place at the end of the nineteenth century; the Sackville opened in 1890, Glyne Hall in 1893, Wilton Court in 1900 and the Metropole the same year. The Granville Hotel was built in 1902 but not opened until 1905. The Bexhill Hotels Association was founded in 1933 and at its peak had a membership of 140.

An increasing population and more visitors created a demand for entertainment. York Hall in London Road was opened in 1895 by Mr J. P. Goodwin, who later built the Pelham Hotel at Sidley. But the first major centre was the Kursaal, opened on the seafront in 1896. Until 1906 it was owned by the De La Warr estate and ornamental gates at the bottom of Sea Road could shut off the site. The Germanic name 'Kursaal' was anglicised as the Pavilion during the First World War, and the building continued in use until its demolition in 1936. Entertainments also took place in Egerton Park, both in the open air and in the hall built in 1903 (this now houses Bexhill's museum). Also in the park was the Pergola, an open-air theatre which was expanded into the Park Theatre, built in 1933. On the seafront was the Colonnade, opened in 1911, which featured a bandstand. The De La Warr Pavilion, situated behind the Colonnade, opened in 1936. This building is now one of the town's principal claims to fame and is regarded as an outstanding example of the 'modernist' art deco style, embodying a new form of construction on a steel framework. It is a Grade I listed building.

The Second World War brought an abrupt halt to the town's life as a resort with the renewed threat of invasion from the continent. Although there was a brief commercial revival after the war, with many taking seaside holidays after six years' deprivation, a gradual decline in Bexhill's prosperity was evident. The opening of new holiday markets abroad, with the prospect of the unfamiliar and the virtual guarantee of sun, undermined the traditional English resort. Trade declined and the hotels began to close, with many being converted into flats to cater for a new focus for the town – as a retirement centre forming part of the south coast's 'Costa Geriatrica'. During the same period most of the larger schools closed and membership of the Independent Schools Association declined to thirteen. Convalescent homes also fell out of fashion, or were subject to cutbacks: the two NHS units were closed. In 1964 the dramatic reduction of the country's railway system saw the loss of the Charing Cross–Crowhurst–Bexhill West line, reducing the town's accessibility. And in 1974 administrative changes saw the disappearance of Bexhill as a separate local government entity; instead the town was pitched together with Battle and surroundings to form the Rother Valley District. Although its population continues to grow (rising from 34,340 in 1981 to 37,063 in 1991), Bexhill is still struggling to find a new role to take the place of its inter-war heyday.

Left: St Peter's Church was the focal point of the town for much of its history, although its site on the hill now seems rather isolated. Although the church has Saxon origins its most notable feature today is its Norman tower, built towards the end of the eleventh century. There is one Saxon legacy in the church – an elaborately carved stone discovered in the nineteenth century under the floor of the nave. This is thought to be the lid of a reliquary (which would hold the relics of a saint). The Norman architecture was largely replaced in the thirteenth century and the medieval church, like many others in the country, was modernised in the nineteenth century when the building was enlarged. The Victorian architect in charge of these alterations was William Butterfield, whose masterpiece was All Saints Church, Margaret Street in London.

Chantry Lane runs from the Old Town northwards towards Sidley. The fact that it is cut deeply between the banks on either side suggests that it follows an ancient track. It commences at the Old Town end with Barrack Hall, part of which was an officers' mess during the Napoleonic Wars when the King's German Legion, under the command of General Charles Von Alten, were stationed at Bexhill (the King of England still at that time being also the Elector of Hanover). Their camp covered about 25 acres and lay between Chantry Lane, Belle Hill (originally Belly Hill) and Barrack Road (hence the name). The registers of St Peter's church record a number of weddings and deaths linked with the garrison. The cemetery in Barrack Road was opened as an extension of the old parish churchyard specifically for deceased members of the garrison. In the 1970s, the Old Town bypass was constructed across Chantry Lane, introducing a concrete 'bridge' two thirds of the way down its length. Thus the tranquil rural scene shown in this picture has disappeared.

An Edwardian view of the High Street in the Old Town. On the left is the shop of Henry Eldridge, fruiterers – the legend 'And at the Gardens, De La Warr Road' is painted on the lower part of the shopfront. Behind Eldridge's is Hanover House, built in 1806, possibly for an officer from the King's German Legion. The shop has now been removed, revealing the full frontage of the house. Hidden behind the trees is Linkwell, built about twenty years later by Richard Day and incorporating an older building dating back to the seventeenth century. More recently the house was lived in by Desmond Llewelyn, 'Q' in the James Bond movies. The row of buildings on the right is a mixture of Georgian and Victorian styles, and the general stores, with the lady walking past, advertises in its window 'Invalid Port'. That shop front has also now been removed. On the extreme right are the premises of Cave Austin, grocers, and F. Ballard, bootmakers.

Manor House, Bexhill.

The original medieval Manor House was used by the Bishops of Chichester as their residence when visiting the eastern end of their see. The Sackville family, given the manor by Elizabeth I, did not use the house regularly (preferring the magnificence of Knole, their main seat). In the nineteenth century the Manor House was occupied by several local families, most notably the Brooks. When Mr A. S. Brook moved to Grange House at the top of Sea Road, the Manor House was bought by Viscount Cantelupe (later 8th Earl De La Warr) as a home for himself and his new bride, Lady Muriel Brassey, whom he had married in 1891. They moved into the renovated house the following year and it became the social centre of Bexhill until their marriage broke down a decade later. In the 1890s the grounds extended to what is now the site of Manor and Magdalen Roads where a cricket ground was laid out. In 1894 the South African touring team played there, followed by the Australian test side two years later. The house had a private telephone exchange six years before the installation of the town's first public exchange in 1898. In 1903 the property was rented to Mr August Neven du Mont, newspaper proprietor, who had close connections with St Mary Magdalene's Church where his painting of the Crucifixion still hangs. He died in 1909 and his widow remained in the house until the outbreak of World War I when her German connections led to her departure. After the war the house was bought by Sir Leicester Harmsworth and when he died his widow and son remained there. Mrs Harmsworth died in 1963 at the age of 95 at which point the Corporation bought the estate for £22,000. In 1968 the house and some of its outbuildings were demolished. The coach house, barn and stables remain grouped around extensive and well-maintained public gardens.

The creation of the seaside resort of Bexhill was largely due to the enthusiasm and energy of two Earls De La Warr, father and son. The 7th Earl initiated the development with the building of the sea wall between Galley Hill and Sea Road to the east of the town. This fronted his own estate. He died in 1896 and was succeeded by his second son (pictured here), his eldest son having been drowned in a yachting accident. The 8th Earl De La Warr continued the expansion of the town in the first decade of the twentieth century – the family have been described as 'territorially dominant' locally at this time. He invested heavily in the creation of the new resort and as a result was twice involved in bankruptcy proceedings. On the outbreak of World War I the 8th Earl was commissioned in the navy but died in 1915 at Messina, Sicily, after being taken ill with rheumatic fever while returning to the Dardanelles campaign.

Dorset Road was created in the late 1890s when Earl De La Warr's agent George Gray laid out roads on that part of the estate which included the cricket pitch. Dorset Road ran north from the railway line across what is now the A259 to Pentland Road. It housed several schools, including the Beehive School and Ancaster Gate, and included the house where Angus Wilson, the author, was born in 1912. The junction that is shown here is with De La Warr Road: the sign on the left advertises a house, 'Braemar', for sale through agents Hampton & Sons. This junction later became the start of the Old Town bypass.

In Victorian England there was a well-established pattern of clergymen founding and running independent schools. Thus the Revd F. R. Burrows was following distinguished predecessors when he brought Ancaster House School to new buildings off Hastings Road in 1898. The school was described in 1901 as having 'Modern Improvements in Sanitary Arrangements and Ventilation'. It was originally for boys, but after Burrows' death in 1908 his widow changed it to a girls' school. This picture shows part of the original buildings – the school's name can just be made out on the top rail of the gate.

The Burrows' daughter, Frances, was headmistress of the girls school for many years and was very active in the town. Among other interests she played a major role in the Girl Guide movement locally. She became an alderman and was created a Freeman of the Borough in 1958. This picture shows the school's dining-room, complete with potted palms. The buildings still exist, but at the time of writing are empty and vandalised, the school having amalgamated with Charters Towers and moved to Woodsgate Park.

Wrest Wood in Wrestwood Road (originally called Haddocks Hill) was built for Sir Edward Malet in 1897. The *Bexhill Chronicle* for 28 April 1899 records: 'He has chosen to make Bexhill his home mainly on account of its salubrious climate and invigorating atmosphere'. Sir Edward was a distinguished diplomat, having been British Ambassador to Berlin, while his wife, Lady Ermyntrude, was a cousin of the 8th Earl De La Warr. The house was built in a seventeen-acre wooded area with carefully landscaped gardens, and a total of 40 staff were employed there. Sir Edward died in 1908 and in his memory Lady Ermyntrude built the Malet Memorial Hall (1913) at the corner of Belle Hill and London Road. In 1927, after her death, Wrest Wood became Lindores School for Girls under the leadership of Miss Freeman. This school had started in Linkwell in the Old Town High Street. It was evacuated during World War II, and in 1946 the premises were taken over by St Mary's School, which still occupies the site today. The picture shows the original house, surrounded by the playing fields of Lindores School. St Mary's have considerably extended the buildings on site.

One indicator of the changing nature of the local economy has been the decline of the forges. Three survived into the twentieth century – in the Old Town, at Sidley and in Little Common. This picture, dating from the 1920s, shows the forge in the Old Town which was located at the top of Sea Road. Jim Wimborne is shoeing a horse belonging to Pocock's the butchers in the High Street. The other man is Mr Wood. Pocock's, 'High Class Meat Purveyor', were one of the oldest established businesses in the Old Town, having opened a butchers and slaughterhouse in the late eighteenth century. From 1801 until closure in 1998, the business occupied the same premises at 24 High Street. The forge continued in operation until the Second World War but was demolished in 1947. The site is now occupied by Forge House.

This tranquil scene at the top of Sea Road near the Old Town dates from early in the last century. The building on the right is The Grange, then the home of the Brook family, unofficial 'squires' of Bexhill. They were founders of the local hunt, called the Harriers, and the hounds were at one time kennelled behind the house. Opposite it was the entrance to the Women's Convalescent Home (illustrated overleaf). The Grange was badly damaged by bombs during World War II but was subsequently restored. Railings are still in place on the left-hand bank but are now made of rather ugly tubular metal.

Convalescent and residential homes have been a feature of Bexhill since the late nineteenth century. The first of these homes was built at the top of Sea Road in 1881 by the Metropolitan Convalescent Institution. The site, formerly Cheeseman's Farm, was also the location of one of the deepest wells supplying water to the town before a piped supply became available in 1888. The Institution was originally founded in London to provide convalescence for patients discharged from hospital, but with no suitable accommodation in which to recover. It followed up the Sea Road home with another built in 1905 at Cooden in the style of a Georgian country mansion. Thereafter the Sea Road site (illustrated here) provided for women and the Cooden home for men. The women's home was damaged by flying bombs during the Second World War. Both premises became part of the NHS in 1948.

This rather posed photograph, with a number of ladies seated symmetrically in the background, shows the highly polished and rather formal-looking sitting room of the women's home. Eventually the NHS outgrew convalescent facilities and both the women's and men's homes closed in the 1980s. Whether this could be attributed to improved social conditions (reducing the need for such provision), or whether financial choices had to be made and convalescence was judged a lower priority is not clear, but their day had passed. The women's home was demolished in 1989 and the site is now occupied by De Moleyn's Close (named after a fifteenth century bishop of Chichester murdered by sailors at Portsmouth!). The same bishop was licensed by Henry VI to: 'Empark 2000 acres at Bexhill and to enclose and embattle his Manor of the same name'. The convalescent home's lodge remains and the external features of the new houses echo its style.

In 1884 a local board of health was constituted for Bexhill; this event marked the beginning of local government in the town. The first chairman was Lt. Col. Henry Lane and when the board became the urban district council in 1895 he was briefly that body's first chairman. In those early days there was no office accommodation for the board. A site for the town hall was purchased in 1893 and Henry Wood, an architect from Hastings, was commissioned to design the building (he was also responsible for St Stephen's Church in Woodsgate Park). The town hall (left) was opened in 1895 by the then Lord Mayor of London complete with his ceremonial coach. It was soon joined by the equally solid and imposing building for the London and County Bank which was completed in 1898 and can be seen on the right of the picture. It is now used as offices, but the initials 'LCB' can still be seen on the weathervane and its original title is clearly discernible along its Buckhurst Road frontage. Also in 1898 a memorial (far left of picture) was erected in the Town Hall Square to Lt. Col. Lane, who had died in 1895. In just over a decade more space was required and an extension to the town hall was built. The foundation stone was laid by the eight-year-old future Earl De La Warr (later sponsor of the eponymous pavilion), whose grandfather was then mayor. The extension was added to the left of the building, which is shown in its original form here. Shortly afterwards, in 1910, the square was enlivened by the opening of the town's first cinema – the Bijou (later the St George's). In its cinematic heyday the town had four cinemas but by the 1950s the St George's (by then the Savoy) had fallen into decline and was known to local youngsters as the 'fleapit'. It closed in 1954, was later demolished and the site is now the garden of the Castle pub.

In the early 1890s the Roman Catholic parish which included Bexhill stretched from Eastbourne to Lydd and inland as far as Wadhurst. A mission was set up in Bexhill in 1893 to be run by priests from the religious order of the Institute of Charity, in whose care the parish still remains. Father Lockhart, who had been a member of the Oxford Movement with John Henry Newman, was the first priest. The building that now serves as the hall was the first chapel; the present Church of St Mary Magdalene was built in 1906–7. This was designed by Arthur Young of London who had also been responsible for the presbytery and chapel. It is in the Early Decorated style and has been described as 'practically a copy of the Church at Alfriston'. Even a century ago ecclesiastical premises were not safe from criminal activity: in the parish diary it is recorded that on 21 May 1894 a robber was caught in the chapel trying to break open the alms box. The entry goes on to say that he was sent to prison for four months. The new church was the location of the first attempt at a public library when in 1912 some 25 books were made available in the porch. This arrangement lasted until 1918 and in its modest way was the precursor of the public library service provided today. In 1908, when the church opened, the original chapel was converted into a church school which occupied the building until 1961 when it was moved into the east wing of Nazareth House. This picture from 1913 shows the first open air procession by the congregation carrying the statue of Our Lady of Lourdes (a gift from Miss Francis, an early benefactor of the parish). The parish diary records 'About 250 persons took part. Very much admired.'

Before the development of Bexhill New Town south of the railway line, Sea Lane was a track leading down to the seashore. In rough weather the sea would sweep up as far as the site of the present St Barnabas Church. The road's character changed after the building of the new sea wall in the 1880s, which stretched from Galley Hill to Sea Road (as it became). In the following decade the road was developed and much of the original architecture remains today. This picture was taken looking north from the seafront. On the left is Albany House with its first floor balcony and projecting roof. The building was remodelled between the wars and given an Art Deco exterior, at which point the balcony was removed. It housed tea rooms at the time and is still a catering establishment today. On the right is the roofline and spire of St Barnabas Church, built in 1890–91 on land donated by the Earl De La Warr. The architect was Sir Arthur Blomfield and the style is Gothic revival.

Sea Road from the corner of Cantelupe Road looking north towards the station. The corner building is the Sydenham House Café, which has been demolished and replaced by Sydenham Court. In his war memoirs Spike Milligan recalls the café as the WVS Forces Corner, open for 'tea, buns, billiards, ping-pong and deserters'. Behind it are the domes of the Granville Hotel, built in 1902 but not opened until three years later because of a dispute over the granting of a bar licence. Latterly rechristened the Grand, this hotel is now closed. The awning on the opposite side of the road with the word 'milk' prominent on it belonged to Sunnymead Dairies at no. 32.

The development of the town and its rapid increase in population – the number of inhabitants more than doubled in the 1890s – brought a need for entertainment facilities. In 1896 the 8th Earl De La Warr built the Kursaal (literally 'health hall'). This was the nearest Bexhill came to having a pier, being constructed over the beach opposite the De La Warr Parade. The Kursaal was opened by the Duchess of Teck (George V's mother-in-law) on Whit Monday 1906. It stood on the De La Warr estate and large ornamental gates (left, foreground) controlled access to the site. In 1913 the East and De La Warr Parades were bought by the Corporation and the gates were removed. The Kursaal was later leased to Mr James Glover (mayor of Bexhill in 1906–7) and was for some years a major focus for entertainment in the town. It was renamed the Pavilion during World War I and demolished in 1936, giving way to the new De La Warr Pavilion. The site is now occupied by the sailing club.

Carlo Hall in Marine Mansions, the block immediately east of the Glyne Hall Hotel, advertised its proximity to the bandstand and Kursaal (whose gardens are illustrated below) and offered as extras 'Fire in Bedrooms, Boot Cleaning and Baths', while also boasting a 'certificate held for perfect sanitation'. Its terms were up to eight shillings per day in season, and seven shillings off-season.

The Sackville Hotel, a prestigious establishment, was opened by Lord De La Warr in July 1890 and one of the early residents was his son, Viscount Cantalupe, who lived there with his wife until improvements to the Manor House were completed in 1892. In 1897 the family sold the Sackville to Frederick Hotels Ltd. who were the owners until 1957. A suite of public rooms was added in 1900 and a lounge and promenade was built along the main frontage in 1920. During World War II the hotel was damaged by bombs. Until its closure in 1960, the Sackville was the flagship hotel in the town, but in 1963 it was sold for conversion into flats. The building remains, but minus its cupola (on the left in this picture) and with the upper section of the turret having been amputated.

The first motor racing trials in England were held in Bexhill on Whit Monday 1902. The 8th Earl De La Warr had a one kilometre track laid out along the East Parade from the foot of Galley Hill to a point opposite the Marine Mansions. It was estimated that 25,000 visitors came to the town for the event. The fastest speed recorded in these first races, by the French ace Leon Serpollet, was 54 m.p.h. Among the 200 competitors was Alfred Harmsworth (later Lord Northcliffe and founder of the *Daily Mail*). His younger brother, Leicester, later bought the Manor House and estate. The following year a local resident objected to the races blocking access to his house and the event was not held. Racing resumed in 1904 and continued until 1907 when the top speed recorded was 73 m.p.h. In that year, however, the Brooklands track was opened in Kent and Bexhill's brief reign was over. A scheme to provide an alternative track between Cooden and Pevensey came to nothing. In this picture two cars are racing towards Galley Hill with the Hotel Riposo in the background. The Riposo was demolished in 1961 to make way for the flats of Cavendish Court.

Central Parade before the arrival of motor traffic. On the left is Roberts Marine Mansions, with Wilton Court Hotel, which opened in 1900, in the centre. On the right in the distance is the Kursaal and, on the extreme right, the Cairo at the eastern end of Marina Arcade. The writer of this card, sent in 1905, tells his correspondent that along the front you can see Hastings and St Leonards 'very plainly' and that 'There's a good cycle track running up by the golf links' (i.e. on the East Parade).

The exterior of Roberts Marine Mansions with Wilton Court Hotel (distinguished by its cupola) beyond. The tram running in front of the mansions was operated by the Hastings & District Electric Tramways Company. Tram services between St Leonards and the Metropole Hotel started in 1906 when the fare for the whole journey was three old pennies. The trams continued to run until 1928 when they were replaced by trolley buses.

The Marine Hotel was built on the corner of Devonshire Road and the Marina in 1895. It was in this building that the campaign for Bexhill's borough status started a few years later – status that was achieved in 1902. The following year John Reynolds Roberts, a prominent London draper, bought the building for conversion into a seaside home for drapery assistants (a similar home was established in Seaford), at which point it became known as Roberts Marine Mansions. The building was badly damaged by bombs during World War II and was demolished in 1954. It was replaced in 1963 by Dalmore Court. This picture shows the well padded and decorated interior of the Marine Mansions, and makes an interesting comparison with the interior of the women's convalescent home (p12).

A 1939 billhead for the Devonshire Dairy on Devonshire Road.

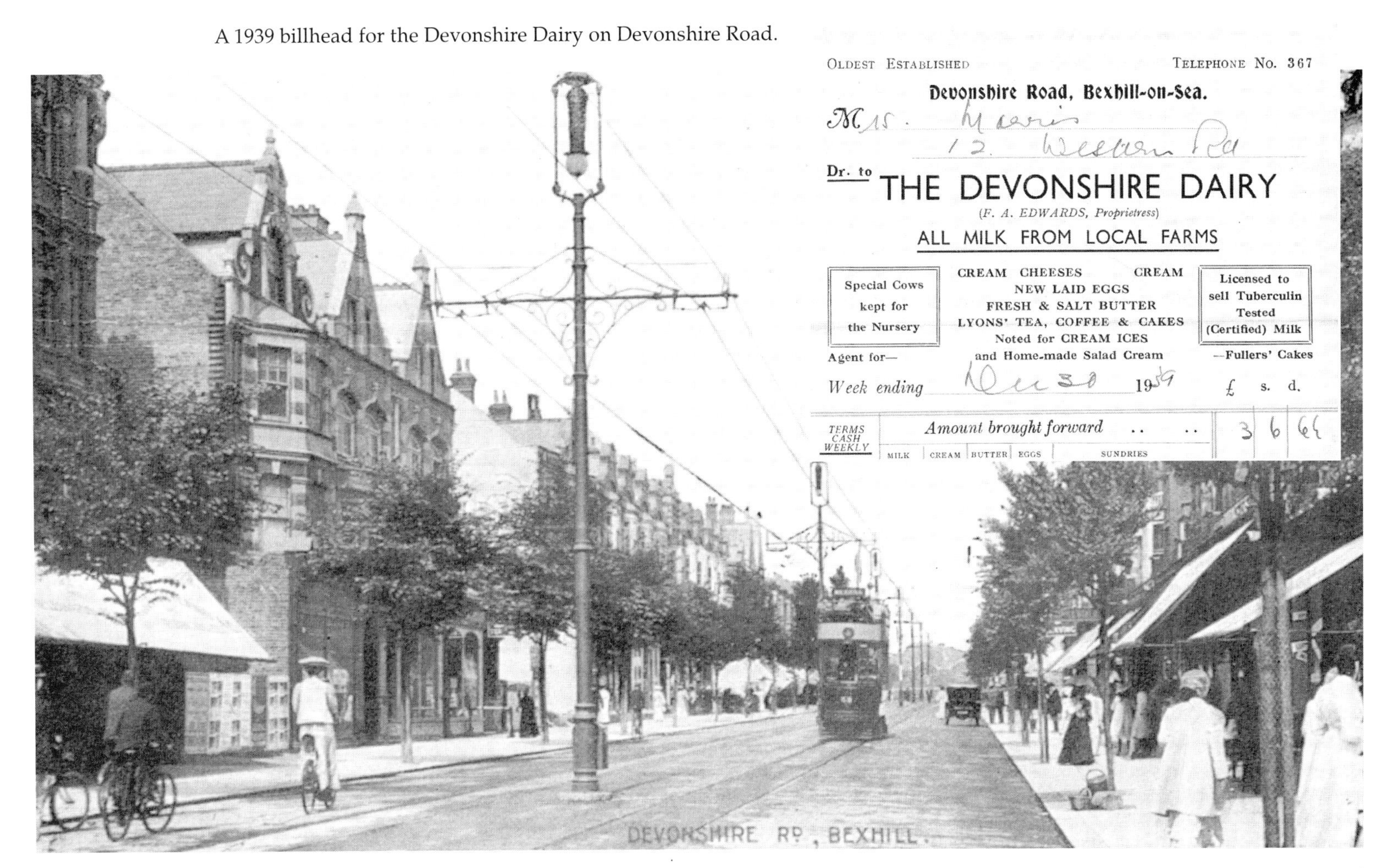

OLDEST ESTABLISHED TELEPHONE No. 367

Devonshire Road, Bexhill-on-Sea.

Dr. to THE DEVONSHIRE DAIRY

(*F. A. EDWARDS, Proprietress*)

ALL MILK FROM LOCAL FARMS

Special Cows kept for the Nursery	CREAM CHEESES CREAM NEW LAID EGGS FRESH & SALT BUTTER LYONS' TEA, COFFEE & CAKES Noted for CREAM ICES and Home-made Salad Cream	Licensed to sell Tuberculin Tested (Certified) Milk

Agent for— —Fullers' Cakes

Week ending 19 £ s. d.

TERMS CASH WEEKLY *Amount brought forward* .. ..

MILK | CREAM | BUTTER | EGGS | SUNDRIES

During the 1890s Devonshire Road rapidly grew into the town's main shopping thoroughfare. John Webb had built the Devonshire Hotel in 1886 and during the next decade no less than three banks opened in the street – a sure indicator of prosperity! The department store Longley's opened in 1906 at no. 59 (on the right hand side of the street as seen in this picture). It expanded steadily, eventually taking in six other adjacent properties and employing up to a hundred people. Bombed in 1942, the premises were rebuilt and older generations remember the pneumatic tube system used in the store for the handling of cash. Longley's closed in 1985. The tramlines dominate the street with the posts used to hold the cables also supporting street lights.

Cooch Behar is now part of West Bengal, but prior to 1950 was one of India's princely states. In the late 1890s the then Maharajah, Nripendra Narayan, visited Eastbourne with his wife and in 1907 took up residence at Moor Hall, Ninfield. In July 1911 the Maharajah was taken ill and it was suggested that he move to Bexhill to enjoy the healthy sea air. A bungalow in Marine Court Avenue was taken for him and he moved there from London. However he continued to decline and died in Bexhill on 18 September 1911. Although his body was taken to London, there was considerable ceremony involved in conveying it from Marine Court Avenue to the station. Military units formed a guard of honour and the band of the King's Royal Rifles accompanied the cortège. The procession travelled up Devonshire Road where all traffic was suspended. As can be seen, shop windows had their blinds down as a mark of respect and hundreds of residents and visitors lined the route.

Within weeks it was agreed that a memorial fountain should be erected in the town to commemorate the Maharajah. The cost was to be borne by the state of Cooch Behar and the memorial chosen was a 14-foot fountain in dull glazed Carrara stoneware, complete with a metal cup on a chain. The fountain was formally opened by the Maharajah's second son on 18 September 1913. It was positioned at the Horn near the seafront behind the Colonnade, but in 1934 when the area was being cleared in preparation for the building of the De La Warr Pavilion it was moved to Egerton Park. Sadly, it was removed in 1963. The buildings behind the fountain in this picture still remain, although the coastguard cottages on the right were demolished to make way for the De La Warr Pavilion.

This view looks westwards towards the Colonnade. At the left is the western end of Marine Court Avenue, where in the last house (no. 22) the Maharajah of Cooch Behar died. On the right in the background is the bulk of the Metropole Hotel; in front of that the buildings that were cleared to make way for the De La Warr Pavilion. The area in the foreground on the right is The Lawn, which was used for public entertainment and is now part of the Pavilion car park. The lettering above the stage shows that the Coronets were performing at the time. They were a concert party led by Pat Kinsella and Mary Collard.

This picture shows the sea frontage of Channel View. The development, built in 1905, took the form of a hollow rectangle. Along its Marina frontage (known as Marina Arcade) it had oriental-style domes matching the Kursaal's architecture. Within the rectangle there was space for a swimming pool, but this was never built. The Colonnade is visible in the far distance on the left, with the Metropole Hotel (almost hidden) to its right and, in the middle, Marina Court – a block of flats opened in 1901 with shops at street level. This was demolished in 1970 and the site is now part of the Pavilion car park.

As the development of the seafront progressed westwards, the town council constructed Central Parade in 1909/10 and then the Colonnade (illustrated here) in 1910/11. The architect was J. B. Wall, who was later mayor of the borough. The Colonnade was built on the site of one of the Martello towers which had been demolished in 1870. It was opened on the coronation day of King George V (22 June 1911) by Lord Brassey. He was created an earl in the king's coronation honours list and had a distinguished career in public service. His wife Lady Brassey was a keen amateur naturalist. In this picture a viewing platform on the left juts out over the beach providing shelter for those underneath.

The Colonnade was a focus for military band and orchestral concerts until the De La Warr Pavilion opened in 1936, and a guidebook of the 1920s described it as 'an unusual but effective concert hall'. This picture shows the Colonnade being used to entertain a rather sparse audience in front of a bandstand that no longer exists. During the Second World War the Colonnade, heavily reinforced with sandbags, served as one of the town's air raid shelters. Today it has a rather wistful air, still stately but pining perhaps after lost eminence.

BOROUGH OF BEXHILL.

THE COLONNADE.

Chairman: Councillor J. B. AVERY. Secretary: Major Geo. TYER.

GRAND BENEFIT CONCERT

SATURDAY, SEPT. 26th, 1925, At 8.15 p.m.

By kind permission of the Bexhill Corporation and under the Distinguished Patronage — of — HIS WORSHIP THE MAYOR, (Councillor R. C. Sewell)

MUNICIPAL ORCHESTRA

A. GARTH-JONES, Musical Director.

SOUVENIR PROGRAMME :: Price Sixpence.

This 1925 concert held at the Colonnade included among its contents a waltz called 'Breezy Bexhill'.

During the 1920s there was considerable discussion in the town about the desirability of building a major new entertainment centre. By 1930 the council had purchased the 'coastguard site' above the Colonnade, and although architects had prepared plans no progress had been made on the ground. In 1932 the 9th Earl De La Warr was elected mayor of the borough. At the time he was a prominent left-wing politician and held junior ministerial office in the Labour and National governments. As mayor he campaigned vigorously for the building of such a centre. And it was he, once the council gave its support, who announced there would be a competition for the design of a pavilion with Thomas Tait, the architect, as assessor. There were 230 entrants to the competition and the winning design, announced in February 1934, was by Erich Mendelsohn and Serge Chermayeff. The modern design caused controversy and bewilderment locally and there were xenophobic protests nationally by fascist organisations complaining about 'foreign' architects. 'Britons, not aliens, shall carry out the task' said *Fascist Week*. A public inquiry opened in April 1934 following the council's application to central government for a loan to construct the Pavilion. The loan was granted but necessitated some cost-cutting to the project.

The solid affluence of Edwardian Bexhill is illustrated in this picture of Marine Crescent, built in the late nineteenth century in the Queen Anne Dutch gabled style. The row of six four-storey properties survives today largely unchanged.

At right angles to Marine Crescent and now facing onto the roundabout at the foot of Sackville Road is the former 'Beach Towers Boarding Establishment'. Since this Edwardian postcard was produced the building has lost its left-hand side and one of its distinctive towers. No attempt was made to ensure that the replacement building mirrored the eclectic architectural style of the original.

The young boy, appropriately dressed in a sailor's suit, stands in shallow water below the Metropole Hotel. This was built between 1897 and 1900 opposite the end of Sackville Road. It was described as being 'lavishly furnished' and was where the Lord Mayor of London stayed in 1906 when he came to open the Egerton Park extension. During World War I it was used by the Canadian Army, and was again occupied by the armed forces in World War II. In 1940 it suffered a serious fire and was bombed the following year. It was demolished in 1955. Thus the De La Warr Pavilion, originally situated between two large buildings, the Metropole and Marina Court, now stands on its own. The cluster of buildings visible on the right in this picture was removed to make way for the Pavilion.

When the railway line was first built through Bexhill in the mid-nineteenth century, it cut off the marshy grazing lands beside the sea. A series of cattle arches was built to allow the herds access under the railway to their grazing. When John Webb developed the western part of that land 40 years later to create the new commercial centre of Bexhill, he used Sackville arch as a key access point. The original arch was reconstructed and extended to form a bridge (seen in the background of this picture) in 1892; this bridge was replaced just over 80 years later. Locals fondly remember occasions when double-decker buses tried to pass under the old bridge, only to discover that it was only suitable for single-deckers! On the left of this picture of Sackville Road is Neale's Library, and next to it, with carcasses on display outside, the Sackville Meat and Poultry Stores. On the right is the spire of the Methodist Church (dating from 1896) and in the right foreground the premises of S. Kenson & Co., grocers and provision merchants. Today, cement rendering and painting has totally obliterated the bold alternating stripes of brick and stonework over the shops which form such a distinctive pattern in this picture.

The sea was both the origin of Bexhill's prosperity as a resort and a potential source of danger and destruction. This picture shows heavy seas washing through the Colonnade deck, then newly erected. When the Colonnade was built – on a site created by cutting back the low cliff known as the Horn – it comprised a bandstand and a semicircular extension that was carried on piers over the beach. This 'deck' was vulnerable to heavy seas and was eventually demolished, leaving a shallow curve in the esplanade to mark its position.

Bathing in front of the West Parade where Buxton's bathing station was based. Note the two bathing machines on the left and the row of huts behind them. Bexhill had been the first resort in Britain to allow mixed bathing, in 1901. Even in this picture, dating from before World War I, it's noticeable that all sunbathers are fully clad; only a few young legs are exposed. Modesty was the order of the day. A lady, writing in 1913, says on a card to her friend: 'It is quite warm this morning and I really should like a dip in the sea, but they haven't got any machines out yet'. Note the three deckchairs in front of the huts, which have canopies. Behind the bathers is the Colonnade with its bandstand and – jutting out over the beach – semicircular deck.

The land that now forms Egerton Park was originally a marshy area fed by a stream flowing from Sidley. John Webb, in his development of the western end of the 'new town' in the 1880s, created the first part of the park, diverting the stream to form a lake there. He provided the first tennis courts in 1889, as well as a swimming bath.

In the late 1880s John Webb, who had constructed the East Parade for the De La Warr estate, developed the West Parade and the Egerton estate. Most of the early hotels were built on the East Parade and Mr Webb concentrated on residential properties for his new venture. Oceania, the house shown in this picture (still standing), was built around 1902/3 and for a long time stood in isolation. The council bought the West Parade from Mr Webb in 1901 and in 1910 heavy storms so damaged the promenade that it had to be rebuilt by the contractor Stephen Carey. The clock tower in front of Oceania was the town's way of commemorating the coronation of Edward VII in 1902, although it was not completed until 1904. The two cars have been identified as a 1904 or 1905 Mors 24 h.p. (foreground) and a 1904 Panhard Levassor.

The park was named after Charles Egerton, a relative by marriage of Earl De La Warr. At the turn of the century the council took it over and began a programme of improvement and extension. A further four acres of land, reaching to Brockley Road, were incorporated into the park and the Lord Mayor of London, Sir W. Vaughan Morgan, with entourage, carried out the official opening in July 1906. A shelter hall (now the museum) was built as a concert hall in the same year, and a bowling green followed in 1907.

For many years the park was the venue for popular theatre performances and reviews, which took place in the Pergola (built in 1906) – later extended into the Egerton Park Theatre, or Pavilion. This programme from the 1938 season lists among the cast Desmond Llewelyn, playing 'Sprules (a Butler)'. Llewelyn was later better known as 'Q' in the James Bond films and lived in the Old Town until his death in 2000.

The swimming baths were created in 1889 when John Webb was developing Egerton Park. He lined an old salting depression with concrete and piped in sea water. The pool was improved and relined several times and survived into the 1980s. Besides being available to the general public, it was used by local schools for their swimming lessons and galas: former pupils remember it as being particularly bracing and recall a grammar school swimming gala when an enthusiastic senior dived spectacularly and parted company with his trunks, embarrassing him but delighting the whole school. This view looks east towards Park Road and part of the park can be seen on the left. To the west of the pool was what was originally the park shelter hall, initially used as a venue for concerts but now Bexhill's museum. The pool site is currently an open paved space but plans are being formulated for an extension to the museum to be built on it.

An important feature of seaside resorts such as Bexhill was the concert party. This 'review' type of live entertainment started in the town in 1900, and performances were given along the seafront and in Egerton Park. The 'Poppies' Concert Party (the name is misspelt on the postcard) was one group that performed for a number of years in the Pergola open-air theatre in the park. Will Tissington and Katharine Craig led the group until World War II brought this era to a close.

EMPIRE DAY, 1927.

In 1912 the Corporation bought thirteen acres of land between Brockley and Richmond Roads from the developer John Webb. Initially this was used as a municipal tip but, having been levelled out, was formally opened as a recreation ground in 1923 providing a bowling green and a football pitch. The Polegrove, as it was called, was also the venue for many large scale open-air events. This picture shows some of the crowd gathered for the celebration of Empire Day, 24 May (the anniversary of Queen Victoria's birthday) in 1927. This coincided with the silver jubilee of the borough and the town's mayor, Sir Ernest Birch, organised a celebratory gathering in the Polegrove. The crowd included as many as 2,000 children, some of whom can be seen in the front rows fully equipped with flags – and identical headgear!

Passengers waiting at Bexhill West station in the early 1900s. As was the case in many places across the country, the arrival of the railway marked the beginning of change. Hitherto relatively remote towns and villages became accessible and opportunities for travel brought with them demand for services and accommodation. In Bexhill the original railway service was a single line between Lewes and Bulverhythe which opened in 1846 – at that time it ran through fields since the old town of Bexhill was located on the hill. The line was extended east to Hastings in 1851 and a spur line to Eastbourne opened in 1871. A new station fronting Devonshire Square was built for the developing town to the south in 1891. The current station was opened in 1902 and the previous buildings were demolished. However, the route to London Victoria via Lewes was not considered direct enough and the Bexhill, Sidley & Crowhurst Railway Company promoted a parliamentary Bill for the construction of a line from Bexhill to join the Charing Cross to Hastings main line at Crowhurst. This Bill was enacted in 1897 and building work, which included the viaduct over the Crowhurst marshes, started the following year. New stations were built at Sidley and at the Bexhill terminus (later known as Bexhill West station) which fronted the new Terminus Road, opening up the Cranston and Collington Estates. The new line opened in 1902 and served the community for over 60 years.

During World War I troops from the allied armies were stationed for training at Cooden, and the Canadian Army had a trench warfare school on the south side of Cooden Drive. The soldier who sent this card in July 1917 writes: 'Here is a snap of the "gang". We do this sort of thing in the afternoons and it is quite a relaxation more or less. We had our first exams yesterday morning and in the afternoon we swanked up and down the promenade in our new uniforms.'

Official proposals to develop the De La Warr estate in Cooden included a plan for a large hotel on Cooden Sea Road. This never materialised, but the Cooden Beach Hotel came into being in 1931 through the conversion of three shops. It was owned by the De La Warr family and saw visits by King George V and Queen Mary in 1935: Lord De La Warr, then mayor of Bexhill, had previously been lord in waiting to the King. Ramsay MacDonald, when prime minister, also stayed there on a golfing holiday. The hotel was later owned by a local family by the name of Shields. Posts supporting the trolleybus cables can be seen in front of the hotel, which was at the western end of the trolleybus service. In May 1994 the hotel was acquired by Jarvis Hotels.

The 8th Earl De La Warr laid out a golf course which was opened in 1912 on part of the old Cooden Manor estate (Cooden is named after the Norman settler John de Coding). Its clubhouse dates from the same time. The establishment of the golf course accelerated the making up of Cooden Drive following the course of the tramway. Twelve years later the course was the setting for the English Ladies' Championship. Harry Benge is remembered as having been greensman for 50 years 'and well he did it'. In 1959 the 9th Earl De La Warr sold the club to a company formed from its members. From this elevation, the clubhouse remains substantially the same today.

The Bexhill Harriers existed for 130 years until their disbanding in 1915. The Brook family (who lived in the Manor House) ran them and their kennels were in the Old Town. Viscount Cantelupe took over the hunt and built new kennels in Cooden in 1891 (his fiancée, the Hon. Muriel Brassey, laid the foundation stone). The Harriers hunted with Southern hounds, a breed now extinct. This horseman, mounted on a grey, is probably the whip, Horace Smith.

The rural nature of Little Common around 1900 is shown in this picture of the village pond. In the middle background is the Wheatsheaf Inn, the only feature remaining today. On the right is the wheelwright's premises, run for many years by the Dicks family. A couple of cartwheels can be seen propped against the side of the building. On the left is the forge where at one time Mr Crocker was the blacksmith. He drew water from the pond to help shrink the iron bands that were fitted to the wheels. Cattle also had access to the pond for watering and in the winter it sometimes froze over and was used as an informal skating rink. Having been filled in, the pond is now the site of the roundabout in the centre of Little Common, which has expanded significantly, especially since the 1960s.

In 1919 Edward Edman Hurst became the first Bexhill resident to be elected chairman of the Hastings County bench of magistrates. Mr Hurst came from an old Eastbourne family which had settled at Ocklynge Manor, and he built a house at Little Common, off Pear Tree Lane, which he named 'Ocklynge'. In his garden he had this replica of Herstmonceux Castle constructed. It was formed in red clay, and was approximately six feet long, two feet wide and three feet high. Some buildings attached to his house survive as Ocklynge Priory but there is no trace of either the pond or this elaborate model.

An early twentieth century picture showing a farmer working a two in hand (a pair of horses) cutting the grass. The Down is an important open space in the borough and was taken over by the council in 1897. Downsborough's map of Bexhill in 1887 shows a cricket ground on the Down even then. It has remained a public recreational area, although in World War II part of it was ploughed up for allotments. The building on the horizon is the Down Mill: this stood on high ground at Glenleigh Park and was owned and managed by the Hoad family. Its life as a working mill ended in the 1920s and it gradually deteriorated, eventually collapsing in 1965. Only the base of the centre post and fragments of millstones remain at the entrance to Old Mill Park. Further to the right is the stocky tower of St Stephen's Church. The original plans for the church, which was consecrated in 1900, included a spire which was never built.

This building was created around an eighteenth century mansion on the western edge of the Down. In 1910 Mrs Neven du Mont, owner of the Manor House and whose husband's family came from Cologne, established in it a school for German boys ('Deutsches Padagogium') whose pupils included a nephew of the Kaiser. The school was short-lived and closed at the outbreak of World War I when its headmaster, Dr Blassneck, was interned. Canadian troops then used the building and an older resident recalls them feeding Belgian refugees who waited outside the school every morning. An ironic twist! Between the wars it was renamed Garth Place and run as a preparatory school by Dr Wanton. During World War II the building was used as the local centre for civil defence services and the meeting place for the town council. In 1946 Miss Fulford opened St Francis School for Girls on the site; one pupil then was Julie Christie, the actress. Following the school's closure in 1972 all the buildings, apart from the entrance arch (dated 1905), were demolished. The site is now occupied by St Francis Close.

COUNTY GRAMMAR SCHOOL FOR GIRLS,
BEXHILL-ON-SEA.

The Governors and Head Mistress request the
pleasure of the Company of

Mr & Mrs. B. J. Cornford.

at the

Distribution of Prizes

by

A. D. C. Peterson, Esq., O.B.E., M.A.
Head Master of Dover College

on Wednesday, 28th November, 1956, at 2.30 p.m.

Alderman Miss A. Claxton, Chairman of the Governors,
will preside.

Kindly present this card
at the door.

R.S.V.P. to the Head Mistress
before November 19th.

The Balfour Education Act of 1902 made local secondary education the responsibility of East Sussex County Council, although the boys' and girls' County Secondary Schools (later the Grammar Schools) in Turkey Road (so-named because of a nearby turkey farm) were not built until 1925–6. Previously children requiring public secondary education had to travel to Hastings, Eastbourne or Lewes. The catchment area included the country districts around the town and each school was designed for 200 pupils. The first intake was in October 1926 and the formal opening took place on 4 February 1927. This was performed by the Duchess of Athol, the only woman holding office in the government at that time.

The original headmaster and headmistress, Mr W. L. Lamb and Miss E. Davis, remained in post for a quarter of a century, seeing the schools through the Second World War when they were evacuated for three years. Among the troops billeted there during the war years was Spike Milligan, who described it as a 'paradise' after a winter under canvas. Although 'semi-detached' architecturally, the schools (and the pupils) remained strictly segregated – with playgrounds separated by a formidable wire and hedge barrier – until 1970 when they were amalgamated into one co-educational establishment. With further developments in education, the buildings became part of the comprehensive system in 1977 and are now known as Bexhill College.

Until the late nineteenth century the town's water supply came from wells, the deepest of which were at Linkwell in the Old Town and at the Sea Road convalescent home. Lord De La Warr outmanoeuvred John Webb, the developer, and set up the Bexhill Water & Gas Company which established waterworks in Wrestwood Road (on the corner of the Wrestwood estate). A piped supply from there became available in 1887. This was augmented six years later by a supply from Sweet Willow Wood, off the Ninfield Road. The Corporation took control of the water company in 1926 and maintained it until 1964 when it was sold to the Eastbourne Waterworks Company. Today the service, again privately run, is provided by South East Water. This picture (reproduced by kind permission of the *Bexhill-on-Sea Observer*) shows the Bexhill councillors' annual visit in 1951 to the Sweet Willow Wood works. While the official reason for such visits was a detailed inspection of the works, what one participant recalls at that time is a lunch of many courses in the poshest local country hotel! The building remains in use, with the initials EWCC clearly visible on one wall. Those pictured in the front row are, left to right: Cllr. Chambers, Mr A. W. Bristow (borough water engineer), Cllr. Mrs Burrell, Ald. H. Allan, Cllr. Len Burch, and Cllr. Trill. In the back row, Ald. Pycroft is to the left of Cllr. Chambers and Cllr. Baker to the right of Mr Bristow. Left of Cllr. Trill is Cllr. Carter and then to his right, Cllr. Alf Stone, Edward Smith (town clerk) and Cllr. Green.

On Norden's map of Sussex, dated 1616, the settlement of 'Sidly' is shown. Sometimes called Sidley Green, the hamlet existed separately until the creeping development of Bexhill swallowed it up. At the end of the nineteenth and in the early twentieth centuries, Sidley expanded, partly in response to the new railway link. As it grew, older features changed and disappeared. Sidley pond, which was situated at the back of the New Inn, was filled about 1910 and became a children's play area. In this picture the pond can be seen with Pond Head Cottages on the far side. In front of the cottages, at the edge of the pond, is the pound where stray animals were kept until their owners claimed them. The cottages, on Glovers Lane, were demolished in the 1950s.

22968 Sidley. Railway Station and Pelham Hotel.

The construction of the branch railway line from Bexhill West to Crowhurst to link up with the Hastings to Charing Cross line brought expansion and prosperity to Sidley with the provision of a local station. Mr J. P. Goodwin, who had already built the York Hotel, constructed the Pelham Hotel opposite the station. A plaque on the building bears the date 1900. Mr Goodwin said at the time that his hotel would provide stabling facilities then lacking in Sidley – an interesting juxtaposition with the new rail transport on the other side of the street! The Pelham Hotel remains but the railway station was closed in 1964 under the Beeching cuts. With exact irony, a petrol filling station now stands on the site. Close to this site Cramp's Farm had witnessed conflict between smugglers and the 'Coast Blockade' (customs men) in 1828 which resulted in several deaths and the deportation of eight smugglers to New South Wales.